REPTILES

John Burton

Iguana

A Golden Photo Guide
from St. Martin's Press

Schneider's dwarf caiman

Red-legged tortoise

Prairie rattlesnake

REPTILES

A Golden Photo Guide from St. Martin's Press

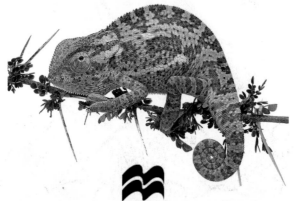

St. Martin's Press

New York

Manufactured in China

Produced by
Elm Grove Books Limited

Series Editor Susie Elwes
Text Editor Angela Wilkes
Art Director Susi Martin
Index Hilary Bird

Original Edition © 2000 Image
Quest Limited
This edition © 2001
Elm Grove Books Limited

**St. Martin's Press
175 Fifth Avenue
New York N.Y. 10010.
www.stmartins.com**

A CIP catalogue record for this
book is available from the
Library of Congress

ISBN 1-58238-179-8

Text and Photographs in this
book previously published in
Eyewitness 3D Reptiles

This edition published 2001

ACKNOWLEDGMENTS
Biofoto Associates:17, 27, 33, 36, 40; **Jane Burton**: 51; NHPA 6, 6, 10, 11, 11, 13, 14, 20, 23, 23,
24, 27, 28, 28, 29, 29, 31, 36, 37, 37, 37, 38, 42, 45, 46, 48, 48, 48, 52, 52; **Tim Hellier**: 4, 7, 9, 39;
Chris Parks:: Title, 5, 7, 9, 11, 12, 14, 15, 16, 19, 20, 21, 23, 25, 27, 29, 31,34, 36, 37,39,40,41,43, 44,
47, 49, 51, 53, Index; **Peter Parks**: 31, 44; **Justin Peach**:Title, 4, 5, 6, 8, 9, 10, 13, 15, 17, 18, 19, 20,
22, 23, 24, 25, 26, 27 ,28, 30, 33, 36, 37, 41, 42, 50, 52, 53, Index; **Jan Taylor**: 42; **Kim Taylor**: 1, 2, 2,
5, 8, 10, 12, 12, 12, 13,16, 30, 32, 32, 38, 38, 40, 44, 45, 46, 48, 48, 49, 50, 55, Index.

CONTENTS

*king
ko

Hatching tortoise

ALL REPTIL

The first reptiles evolved from amphibians during the Carboniferous era, about 340 million years ago. Unlike amphibians, however, reptiles do not have to return to water to breed. Four main groups of reptiles exist today, the *chelonians*: turtles and tortoises; the *crocodilians*: crocodiles, alligators, caimans, and gavials; the *rhynchocephalians*: tuataras, the sole modern survivors of this early order of reptiles; and the *squamatae:* snakes and lizards.

Africa's royal python grows to a length of 5 feet (1.5 m).

SNAKES

Snakes are long, legless reptiles. They are found on every continent except Antarctica. Most snakes live on land, but some inhabit the world's oceans. Snakes are predators – they feed on a variety of mammals, other reptiles, birds, and eggs.

CHELONIANS

Tortoises and turtles are shelled reptiles that live mainly in warm and hot climates. They have changed little since they first appeared 200 million years ago. Tortoises are land-dwelling reptiles, while turtles live in water.

Herman's tortoise

DINOSAUR EGGS
Fossilized dinosaur eggs are similar to the eggs of many modern reptiles and some large modern birds. Modern birds are probably the closest descendants of the dinosaurs.

LOTS OF LIZARDS
The most widespread reptiles are the lizards. There are more than 3,000 different species, from tiny geckos to bizarre chameleons and large monitors. There are a few species of legless lizards, which closely resemble snakes.

CROCODILIANS
Modern crocodiles are very similar to their ancient relatives, which lived at the same times as the dinosaurs. Many ancient crocodiles grew to an enormous size larger than the crocodilians of today.

Young crocodiles have small teeth and often eat insects.

The long tail helps the lizard to keep its balance.

The lizard's speed depends on its strong hind legs.

Long toes with sharp claws

Water dragon

COOL CHARACTERS

Reptiles are cold-blooded animals. This does not mean that their blood is cold, but unlike birds and mammals, they cannot develop their own heat by chemical reactions inside their bodies. Instead their temperature is determined by their surroundings. Their method of controlling their body temperature is to bask in the sun to absorb heat and move to the shade, into water, or even underground to cool down.

Pet tortoises need a cool, dry place to hibernate.

WINTER SLEEP
In tropical regions, tortoises are active the whole year round. Those kept in colder climates hibernate during winter, a type of deep sleep, until the temperature rises.

SUN BAKING
Nile crocodiles bask in the sun to warm up if they are cold. In the intense midday sun, they lie in the water or shelter in burrows to prevent themselves from overheating.

Crocodiles bask together in peaceful groups on the banks of a river.

PUFF ADDER
Tropical snakes, such as this puff adder, are often active at night, when it is cooler. They hide from the intense daytime heat in dark caves, hollow trees, and underground holes.

Spiky flaps of skin give off heat to the surrounding air.

OPEN-MOUTHED
The lizard opens its mouth so its watery saliva can evaporate and help cool it down.

WRAPPED UP TIGHT
This python can only digest its food when it is warm. It curls itself into a ball after eating to retain the maximum amount of body heat.

KEEPING BABY WARM
The young of common lizards, one of Europe's most northerly species, are born black to help them absorb the maximum heat from the sun's rays. Their mother's skin is camouflaged to blend in with their grassy habitat.

BRIGHT GREEN
The vivid coloring of the Madagascan day gecko is in the lower layer of skin, the dermis. The epidermis, a translucent top layer of skin, covers and protects it.

SKIN & SCALES

Many reptiles are covered by a thin skin that forms a waterproof barrier, stopping moisture from getting in or out of the reptile's body. Thin-skinned reptiles frequently shed their skin. A new layer of skin grows beneath the old one. Thicker-skinned reptiles are armor-plated against an attack by their predators.

The scales are smaller on the most flexible areas of the body.

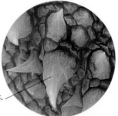

Spiked scales protect the lizard from predators.

CROCODILE SKIN
A crocodile has a tough, leathery skin with large, bony scales on its back.

LIZARD SKIN
The bearded dragon of the Australian deserts has spiked scales under its throat to make it look fierce.

SMOOTH AS GLASS
The European glass snake takes its name from its smooth, shiny skin. It is closely related to the slow worm, which is a legless lizard.

Round tongue

SNAKESKIN CLOSE UP
Snakes have a layer of smooth dry skin covering their over-lapping scales. This rattlesnake has scaly brow ridges to protect its eyes. The hole below its eye is a heat-sensing pit the snake uses to detect the body heat of small mammals.

Python scales form intricate patterns.

SNAKESKIN
This python has small, regular scales on the top of its body.

SHINGLEBACK LIZARD
This Australian lizard has tough, thick scales and a shiny skin to prevent it from drying out in its desert habitat.

FACE-TO-FACE

A reptile's face is adapted to its particular way of life. Its sharp teeth may be seen when its mouth is shut or its jaws curve up in a smile. Its head may be surrounded by an expandable hood, or a threatening frill. It may appear to have horns. The bob-tailed skinks appear to have two faces because their tails resemble their heads as an elaborate camouflage.

LONG JAWS
The gavial, an Asian river crocodile, has long, narrow jaws lined with pointed teeth. It sweeps its jaws from side to side in the water to catch fish.

The softer skin of the head and legs is often colored for camouflage.

HEAD OUT
A tortoise can withdraw its head into the protection of its shell. Tortoises are herbivores; their toothless beaks bite into leaves and other vegetation. Their well-developed eyes are protected by heavy lids. Tortoises have no external ear flaps or openings, and cannot hear very well.

HORNED SNAKE
Several species of desert-dwelling vipers have a horn on their face. No one knows the purpose of the horn, but it may keep sand clear of their nostrils.

FRILLED LIDS
These extra frilly, scaly eyelids may protect the adder's eyes when it burrows in sand.

This common iguana is shedding its old skin.

HAPPY SMILE
In spite of the fringe of prickly scales along its spine and the spiky flap under its chin, this iguana looks as though it is smiling happily because of the shape of its jaw.

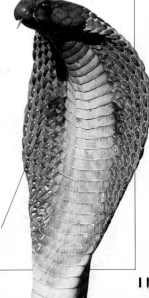

INDIAN HOODS
The cobra has a small face, but when it is threatened it spreads out its hood to make it appear more menacing. It rears up at the same time, hissing aggressively to warn off predators and defend itself.

The snake forms its hood by flattening the ribs on its neck. It makes the upper part of the snake's body seem suddenly much larger.

11

Each eye is set in a scaly cone.

EYE-SPY

Except for some burrowing species, most reptiles have good eyesight and some see in color. A few are blind. Most snakes rely on their eyes both for hunting and for avoiding predators. Instead of movable eyelids, some reptiles have transparent, protective skin coverings over their eyes.

SWIVEL EYES

A chameleon can rotate its eyes to look in any direction. Each eye can move independently; while one eye watches for danger, the other tracks its prey. Using both eyes together, a chameleon can judge distances very accurately.

ROUND-EYED REPTILES

The common iguana is similar to other diurnal reptiles, which are active during the day, and have round pupils. It is also among the reptiles that are known to see in color.

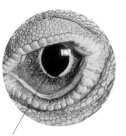

Large eyes see well.

UP PERISCOPE!
A crocodile can lie submerged in water but see clearly all around because its eyes are on top of its head. Crocodiles cannot see well under water.

Pupil closes to a slit in the bright daylight.

Pupil opens wide at night to let in maximum light.

EYE SEE
A caiman's eye has upper and lower eyelids and a third transparent lid that protects its eye underwater. This enables it to keep its eyes open when it dives and swims.

BLIND SNAKE
A blind snake's skin-covered eyes only distinguish between light and dark.

Skin-covered eye

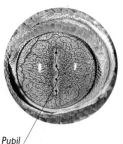

Pupil

BRIGHT PUPIL
In bright light, the notched pupil of a gecko's eye closes to a row of pinpoints.

GLASSY STARE
A green tree snake's eyes have a single, immovable eyelid called a spectacle.

Dust on eyelid

SOUNDING OFF

Snakes are deaf – they have no external ear openings or eardrums to register sound waves. However, they can feel sound vibrations through their jawbones. Pit vipers and some tree-dwelling snakes feel for prey with facial heat sensors.

Most lizards and crocodiles have ear holes and their hearing is good. Reptiles with the best hearing have the widest range of communicating calls.

Snakes can feel sound vibrations passing through their lower jawbone, but they can't locate the direction from which the vibrations are coming.

DEATH ADDER
The death adder's camouflage make it invisible. If disturbed by movements close by it will strike in self-defense. Its bite can be deadly, and usually the victim has been unaware of the danger.

The tip of the tail twitches to lure small rodents within striking distance.

HOT SPOTS
This python has five heat-sensitive pits on each side of its face. It hunts successfully at night, feeling the warmth of prey it cannot see or hear.

The heat-sensitive pit lies between the scales.

HEAT-SEEKERS
Pit vipers hunt with heat-sensitive detectors below their eyes that locate the body heat surrounding small mammals.

The gecko moves its head to locate sound.

GECKO
The gecko makes loud noises to warn others to keep away from its territory. Geckos are the noisiest lizards.

A flap covers the caiman's ear when it is under the water.

CROCODILE CALLS
Crocodilians, such as this young caiman, have a well-developed sense of hearing. They can make a range of sounds, including territorial roars, distress calls, and warning snarls.

The eardrum is not protected by an external flap of skin.

TASTING THE AIR

Snakes and lizards constantly flick out their tongues, "tasting" the air. The tongue collects odors and transfers them to an extremely sensitive detector, the Jacobson's organ inside the mouth. Scents are described as "tastes" because the Jacobson's organ is inside the mouth. Reptiles can scent out all sorts of information about food, water, mates, predators, atmosphere, and land surfaces.

LEAF-LICKING LIZARD
The common iguana samples the smells from plants to find if they are edible. Adult iguanas are vegetarian, but the young eat insects as well as plants.

RIGHT AND LEFT
Each fork of this Brazilian snake's tongue can detect different tastes. Some snakes use their sense of taste to locate a mate as well as to hunt for food.

A tiny opening between the jaws allows the tongue to flick in and out even when the mouth is closed.

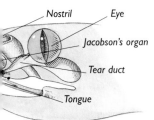

Nostril Eye

Jacobson's organ

Tear duct

Tongue

JACOBSON'S ORGAN

A snake collects airborne
chemical particles on its
tongue and transfers them
to its Jacobson's organ. This
is a nerve-rich pit in the
roof of its mouth. The
Jacobson's organ analyzes
what the tongue collects
and sends messages to the
snake's brain.

*Skinks find other skinks by
"smelling" them with
their tongues.*

AUSTRALIAN SKINK

This lizard uses its
bright blue tongue
to "smell" out food,
mates, rivals, and
predators. Birds
successfully catch
skinks by swooping
before the lizard
"smells" them.

LONG-RANGE MONITOR

Monitor lizards "smell" carrion
"dead animals" using their long
tongues. Some monitor
species can detect the
scent of decaying flesh
as much as 6.8 miles
(11 km) away.

*Most lizards have an undivided tongue,
but the monitor lizard's tongue is forked
like a snake's.*

BARE BONES

Reptiles vary enormously in appearance, but their skeletons have a similar arrangement. Most reptilian skeletons are composed of lots of individual bones. The bones provide attachments for muscles and support the weight of the heavy, muscular body. The skeleton also protects the body's internal organs.

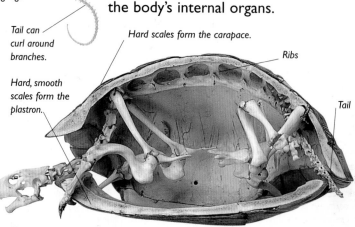

Long legs

HANGING ON
The chameleon has longer legs than most lizards and its feet and tail are adapted for holding firmly on to branches.

Tail can curl around branches.

Hard, smooth scales form the plastron.

Hard scales form the carapace.

Ribs

Tail

TORTOISE STRUCTURE
A tortoise shell has two layers, the hard outer layer of scales and an inner layer of bone. Most vertebrae and the ribs are fused to the shell.

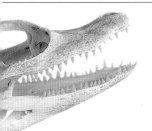

DEADLY GRIP
A python's jaw is joined by long ligaments and can be opened wide enough to allow it to swallow large prey. Backward-curving teeth hook the victim down the snake's throat.

Rows of sharp teeth grip prey tightly.

CROCODILE HEAD
The huge eye sockets are set at the top of the crocodile's skull.

PYTHON SKELETON
Snakes evolved from lizardlike ancestors, but lost their limbs in the process. Snakes can have more than 400 individual vertebrae in their spines, making their bodies very flexible. A pair of ribs arches out from each vertebra, except for those in the tail.

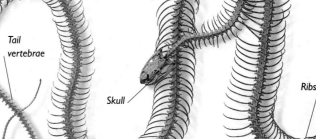

Tail vertebrae

Skull

Ribs

SNAKE MOVES

Snakes are legless. They move their bodies forward or sideways in four different ways: serpentine motion, rectilinear motion, concertina motion, and sidewinding. Most snakes usually employ serpentine motion, although they can also move by one of the other methods.

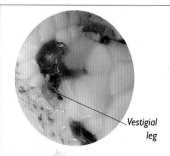

Vestigial leg

LITTLE LEGS!
Boa constrictors and a few other snakes have vestigial legs, small, clawlike traces of hind legs at the base of the tail.

SERPENTINE MOTION
The snake anchors its body against several points on the ground, and then pushes its body forward with its muscles in S-shaped curves.

Vipers, such as this Asian pit viper, use both serpentine and rectilinear motion.

RECTILINEAR MOTION
In this creeping movement, the snake pulls itself along using special scales on its belly. The belly scales hook into rough ground, and the snake drags its body forward.

Muscles raise and flatten the belly scales.

Muscles pull the body into an S shape.

SIDEWINDING

Some desert snakes move by throwing their bodies clear of the ground in a series of sideways movements. This is called sidewinding. It stops the snake from slipping on shifting sand.

S FOR SERPENT

The typical S shape of a snake moving with a serpentine motion. The snake pushes itself forward from the bend of each curve in a swift, flowing movement that appears effortless.

CONCERTINA 1, 2, AND 3

The snake moves by bunching its body up into concertinalike folds and then straightening out.

1 The snake anchors its head to the ground and muscle contractions ripple down the body.

2 The front moves forward and the middle contracts.

3 The middle straightens out and the tail end contracts.

HANGERS AND GLIDERS

Arboreal lizards and snakes spend their lives in the trees. Typically they have prehensile tails, specially adapted tails that they can wrap tightly around a branch. Anchored by their tails, some snakes are strong enough to hold themselves unsupported in midair to strike at prey or move to another tree. Several lizards have evolved special flaps and webs of skin that enable them to glide, but not to fly, from tree to tree.

The thin tip of the tail is knotted securely around a branch.

The snake's body reaches out to another branch and coils around it before it releases its tail anchor.

HANGING LOOSE

Cook's tree boa is a nocturnal tree-dwelling snake that feeds mostly on birds and bats. It strikes out at its prey while keeping a tight grip on a branch.

The boa catches its prey in its strong jaws, and coils its body around its victim.

FREE FALL!
The gecko leaps toward a lower branch, spreading its webbed feet and side skin flaps as it glides down.

EXTRA GRIP
A chameleon's tail helps it to balance as well as to move to another branch. Its tail can also grip branches to steady the whole animal when, with its amazing sticky tongue, it makes a lightning strike at its insect prey.

Suspended by its tail, the chameleon can swing forward.

The Asian flying lizard folds its "wings" away by its sides.

Large snakes are muscular and heavy and require a firm support.

A HIGH STRIKE
A pit viper can only strike downward and sideways. It forms a triangular base with its lower half to support its muscular body.

FLYING LIZARDS
The "wings" of Asian flying lizards are colorful flaps of skin supported by elongated ribs. They allow the lizards to glide long distances.

LEG WORK

Reptiles with four legs do not stand upright with their legs supporting their bodies from underneath like other quadrupeds. Reptile legs sprawl at their sides, only semi-supporting their bodies. They often rest their bodies on the ground between steps when moving slowly. The effort of raising their bodies to move fast can only be sustained over short distances.

SLINKY SKINK
A skink walks, moving its diagonally opposite legs at each step like other quadrupeds. It appears to scuttle when moving fast.

The left hind foot and the right fore foot move forward at the same time.

ISLAND GIANTS
Giant tortoises move so slowly their survival depends on a good food source and living where there are no predators.

These massive tortoises can weigh up to 202 lb (90 kg).

The body bends to the right.

LIZARD LEAP

The Australian frilled lizard's long-toed, clawed hind feet allow it to grip firmly and leap clear of danger.

BASILISK LIZARD

The basilisk is also known as the Jesus Christ lizard. This is because its long, fringed toes spread the lizard's weight and enable it to run across water to escape from danger.

The frill stands up when the lizard opens its mouth wide to threaten predators or to attract females.

SWIMMING IN SAND

When moving through grass or sand, some skinks "swim" by waggling their bodies while keeping their tiny legs quite still.

The right hind foot and left fore foot move forward next.

The body bends to the left.

The sequence of movement is then repeated.

Hind legs are the strongest.

FANCY FEET

Reptile feet are all shapes and sizes, but they share a basic structure of five digits or toes. Lizards' feet are adapted with webs and claws for swimming, tree climbing, and digging. The gecko has scaly toe pads that give it the remarkable ability to grip smooth surfaces, even when suspended upside down. Crocodilians' feet have webs for swimming and claws for gripping and scraping. The flippers of turtles have the same five-digit structure.

A close-up of the gecko's foot reveals that the toe pads have a series of flexible ridges that lock the foot on to smooth surfaces. Sharp claws give extra grip.

Huge belly scales

Flap of skin for gliding

FLYING FEET
This gecko lives in rain forests in Southeast Asia. It can glide between trees using its webbed feet and the flaps of skin along its body. It has gripping pads on its toes that enable it to cling to a smooth leaf surface at the end of a "flight."

The toes on the chameleon's front feet are divided into two groups for a better grip.

WRAPAROUND TOES

A chameleon's front feet have two toes on the outside and three on the inside. This arrangement of toes enables the feet to encircle a branch firmly and hold the chameleon quite still as it hunts. Chameleons move very slowly.

Long toes end in sharp claws.

Webbed feet

Clawless paddles

LONG TOES
Most lizards have long toes with sharp claws at the end. One toe on the hind foot is usually very long.

BIG FOOT
Crocodiles have webbed feet for steering and paddling in the water. The large claws scrape hollows and nests on the bank.

PADDLE-FOOT
The green turtle's flippers are strong swimming paddles. The turtle can reach speeds of 17 mph (28 km/h) underwater.

WATER WORLD

Many reptiles are perfectly at home in the water, and some are expert swimmers. Sea snakes feed, sleep, breed, and give birth in the oceans. They can stay underwater for hours without needing to surface. Female marine turtles come ashore for only one night each year to lay their eggs; otherwise, like the males, they spend their entire lives at sea.

DIVING LIZARD
The marine iguana of the Galápagos Islands is the only lizard species that feeds in the sea. It gnaws seaweed and other algae off submerged rocks.

The caiman swims by swishing its tail to and fro.

Rear feet are webbed, for steering and paddling slowly.

DOUBLE VISION
A young Schneider's dwarf caiman swims with its eyes above and below the water. When it dives, it can seal its ears, nose, and throat.

MANGROVE MONITOR
This large lizard is equally at home in the trees, on land, or diving into water.

GREEN TURTLE
A green turtle swims with its oarlike front flippers, and uses its rear flippers for steering. On land it pulls itself along, using its front flippers.

RIPPLE PATTERNS
The terrapin, a freshwater turtle, has patterns on its neck and underside that resemble a rippling water surface. It is well camouflaged for its natural habitat in the sunlit shallows of murky green water.

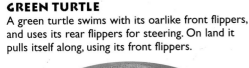

Webbed feet for swimming

A SEA OF SNAKES
The olive sea snake spends its life below the waves. Instead of laying its eggs, it retains them inside its body and gives birth to live young.

The snake swims with an S-shaped motion of its broad, flattened body.

The bright pattern warns that this lizard is poisonous.

FANGS AND VENOM

Venom is a poisonous fluid produced by some snakes and lizards. It is delivered through the reptile's fangs when it bites its victim. Venom can kill or paralyze. Some venoms make the poisoned flesh easier to digest. Some snakes have fangs at the front and others at the back of their mouths. Vipers have hollow fangs that fold down. Not all snakes with fangs are venomous.

The fangs swing down and straighten.

POISONOUS LIZARDS

There are only two species of venomous lizard – the Gila monster and the beaded lizard. Both are found in southern USA and Mexico. The Gila monster chews its venom into its victims. It is rarely fatal to humans.

HARD STRIKE

This copperhead strikes with lightning speed. It opens its mouth very wide and can no longer see its target. Its fangs swing forward for the bite.

When not in use, the fangs are folded back along the jaw in folds of flesh.

If a fang breaks, another grows to replace it.

A spitting cobra has downward-pointing fangs. When the cobra strikes, a jet of air comes out of its throat and sprays venom forward.

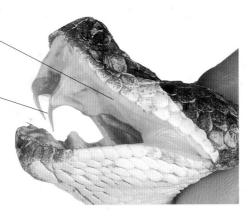

MILKING VENOM
The snake is squeezed gently near its jaws, forcing it to open its mouth and engage its fangs and produce drops of venom. Most venom regularly collected is used to make an antidote to combat the effects of snakebites.

SPITTING MAD
The black-necked spitting cobra sprays venom in the direction of the eyes of a predator. Venom in the eye can cause great pain and usually leads to temporary blindness. The snake spits in self-defense if it is cornered, not to catch prey.

Fang hole

Rat snake's head.

BIG MOUTH

Some snakes can open their mouths and stretch their skin wide enough to swallow prey very much larger than themselves. Most big-mouthed snakes are constrictors. They wrap themselves around their prey to suffocate it. Some constrictors kill venomous snakes.

TIGHT SQUEEZE
The rat snake seizes its prey and rapidly loops around it. Each time the prey breathes out, the snake tightens its grip, until its prey has no room to inhale and suffocates.

As a rat snake swallows, its throat stretches to allow the whole animal inside its mouth. It brings its windpipe to the front of its mouth, so it can continue to breathe while it is swallowing.

This snake is preparing to eat an egg that is much bigger than its own mouth.

DEADLY BITE
This whip snake holds a lizard in its jaws as it waits for the mild venom of its bite to take effect.

EATING EGGS
This egg-eating snake has spikes projecting inside its its throat. The spikes pierce the eggshell. The snake can then crush the shell with its muscles, squeezes the contents down its throat, and regurgitates the shell.

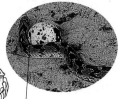

The snake's elastic skin will have to stretch to its limit to engulf the egg.

Large, backward-pointing teeth hook prey down the gullet.

PYTHON SKULL AND JAW
The ligaments of the snake's jaws allow it to open its mouth wide enough to swallow large prey.

The upper jaw is loosely attached to the rest of the skull by ligaments.

The lower jaw is made up of two separate bones, joined by a flexible ligament.

SNAP HAPPY

Crocodiles and other reptiles that kill large animals for food have to tear them into small pieces to eat them because they cannot swallow them whole. Many small reptiles feed on insects and animals they can gulp down without chewing. Herbivorous reptiles often have beaks without teeth and must roll tough vegetation around in their mouths to break it down before swallowing.

PRICKLE-PROOF
The land iguana from the Galapágos Islands feeds mostly on the fruit and leaves of the prickly pear, which it works around in its mouth until the prickles break off.

No teeth are visible when an alligator's mouth is shut.

ALLIGATOR SNACKS
The Mississippi alligator eats fish, snakes, turtles, birds, and crustaceans.

Having snapped up a small insect with lightning speed, this lizard waits for its prey to cease struggling before it gulps it down. The lizard's small teeth are no use for grinding up its food.

Most lizards have small lower teeth to grip their prey firmly.

KILLER DRAGON
Komodo dragons are the largest living lizards. They feed in groups, killing their prey with a number of savage bites.

The larger teeth on a crocodile's lower jaw are still visible when the jaws are shut.

CROCODILE SMILE
Crocodiles often drag large prey into the water to drown it. They may store the carcass underwater and leave it to soften and rot before tearing it up. A crocodile's stomach contains bony fragments to help grind food into digestible pieces.

BEAKS AND TAILS

Tortoises and turtles have toothless jaws and horny beaks. Carnivorous turtles have developed a range of baits and lures to attract fast-swimming fish into their mouths. The matamata turtle relies on suction power to draw in the fish. Some snakes use the tips of their tails to enticing curious prey within striking distance.

METHODICAL MUNCHER

Hermann's tortoise has a vegetarian diet. It bites small pieces from plants with its powerful jaws. It chews each mouthful well before swallowing it.

COME HITHER

Several species of snake, including pit vipers such as this pipe snake, wriggle their tails to attract the attention of prey. The snake strikes when a curious creature comes close to investigate.

This pipe snake waves its red-tipped tail to entice curious lizards to come within its range.

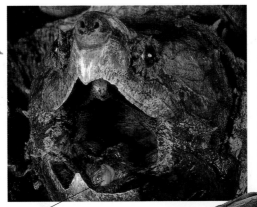

SNORKEL NOSE
This soft-shelled turtle lies like a stone in shallow water, breathing, at the surface, through its snorkel-like nose. Fish that swim over the "stone" are quickly snapped up.

The matamata's shell has peaks to make it resemble an underwater rock.

A wriggling, red, wormlike flap of skin attracts fish between the turtle's jaws.

DEADLY SNAPPER
The alligator snapping turtle has a voracious appetite and eats anything it can catch. It will even grab ducks by their feet and drag them under the water. These reptiles can clear a pond of all other forms of animal life.

SUCKED IN
Disguised as a rock on the riverbed, the matamata turtle lies in wait for its prey. When a fish swims within range, it expands its throat, creating a current that sucks the fish into its mouth.

Alligator snapping turtle

37

STICKY TONGUES

Chameleons have the most amazing tongues. With lightning speed, they can fire their long, muscular, tubular tongues at insect prey. Chameleons rarely miss their target. The insect is engulfed by the tongue and glued to the sticky pad at its end. The chameleon draws it rapidly back into its mouth. Except for its swiveling eyes, all the chameleon's other movements are very slow.

LEAPING LIZARD
This rock agama can spring high into the air to catch insects with its short tongue.

SHARPSHOOTER
A chameleon waits motionless for insects to come within range, then shoots out its sticky tongue with deadly accuracy.

The force of the impact wraps the tongue around the prey.

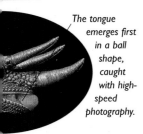

The tongue emerges first in a ball shape, caught with high-speed photography.

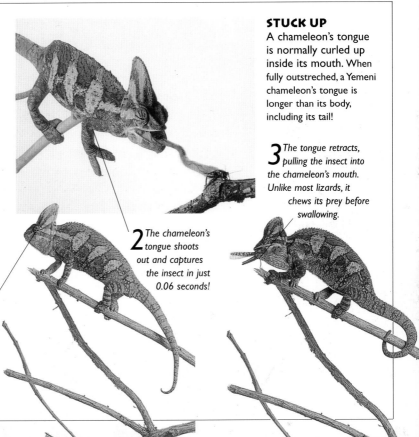

STUCK UP
A chameleon's tongue is normally curled up inside its mouth. When fully outstreched, a Yemeni chameleon's tongue is longer than its body, including its tail!

3 The tongue retracts, pulling the insect into the chameleon's mouth. Unlike most lizards, it chews its prey before swallowing.

FAST FOOD
This Jackson's chameleon is opening its jaws, ready to strike at an insect.

2 The chameleon's tongue shoots out and captures the insect in just 0.06 seconds!

1 A chameleon stands perfectly still as it waits for insects to come by. It can track its prey with its swiveling eyes without moving its head. When it has accurately judged the distance, it strikes.

CAMOUFLAGE

Many reptiles have developed patterns and colors on their skin to help them blend into the background. This camouflage helps them to hide from predators or lie unseen as they wait to ambush prey. Some lizards, including chameleons, can change their color to match the surroundings; others turn a lighter or darker tone.

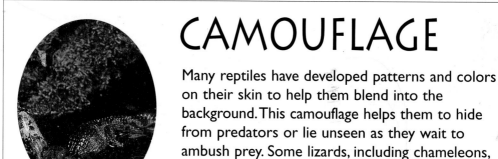

LYING IN AMBUSH
Concealed as a floating stick, this caiman is waiting to pounce on passing animals such as lizards, snakes, birds, and small mammals.

IN THE WIND
A chameleon not only changes color to match its surroundings, but it also sways in the breeze to complete its disguise as part of a branch.

LEAFY LIZARD

Several tree-dwelling geckos mimic the patterns of leaves or tree bark. These geckos hunt by day, so their camouflage conceals them from predators and prey alike.

LEAF LITTER

This venomous snake is a night hunter that preys on small mammals. During the day it is well disguised and warm amongst the leaf litter on the forest floor. It is not an aggressive snake, but it will attack if it is unwittingly disturbed.

Defensive tail spines give the lizard a jagged outline, making it difficult for predators to identify it as a lizard.

SUN AND SHADE

To evade predators, this desert-dwelling North African lizard lightens or darkens its color to merge with its surroundings. Pale tones hides it against the desert sand, while darker tones conceals it in the shade of a rock.

The lizard instantly changes its color as it moves from shadow to sunlight.

GREAT ESCAPES

Many venomous snakes have bright warning colors. Several nonvenomous snakes mimic these colors and patterns to deceive their predators into seeing them as the venomous species and leaving them alone. Reptiles have developed many other ways of confusing predators, including playing dead, discarding their tails, and even sticking out their tongues!

GO AWAY
When threatened, this skink flashes its bright blue tongue to frighten attackers. It is often successful.

TOP OR TAIL?
The Australian bobtailed skink has a tail that looks like its head. This often confuses its predators long enough to allow the lizard to get away.

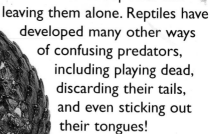

Tail   *Head*

Birds that prey on reptiles seize them behind the head. If the bird grabs this skink's tail instead of its head, it has a chance of surviving the attack.

WHODUNIT

A grass snake lolls, upside down with its mouth open, pretending to be dead. This deters its predators, who will not attack a dead animal.

MISTAKEN IDENTITY

The bright colors of this non venomous milk snake mimic those of the venomous coral snake. It fools predators, who mistake it for a coral snake.

The snake coils around small rodents and rabbits and suffocates them.

DISPOSABLE TAIL

This lizard, like many others, can escape from predators by leaving its tail behind. The discarded tail distracts the predator by continuing to twitch, while the lizard escapes. A new tail soon grows to replace it.

The new tail is never as good as the old one, as it lacks the supporting bones of the original.

43

SELF-DEFENSE

Reptiles have many methods of defending themselves, although usually they try to slip quickly away and hide. However, some reptiles, especially when cornered, will attack in self-defense. The spitting cobra shoots venom at its attacker's eyes. Other reptiles flash their brightly colored tongues or skin flaps and some rattle their tails. Some play dead. A few species of geckos bark loudly. By briefly startling their attacker, they win themselves enough time to make their escape.

TOKAY
The tokay is named after the sounds of one of the calls it makes. If danger threatens, the tokay barks loudly to frighten its attacker.

A new segment is added to the rattle every time the snake sheds its skin.

DEADLY RATTLE
The rattlesnake uses the rattle on the end of its tail to warn predators to keep away. If that does not work, it rears up aggressively. Only when all else fails does the snake attack with its fangs.

INDIAN COBRA

When the Indian cobra is threatened it rears up and spreads its hood. Normally the hood flaps lie flat against its body.

The hood has markings like false eyes to protect the snake from behind.

THRILLING FRILLS

By opening its mouth to gape at an intruder, this Australian lizard makes its frilly collar of skin around its neck stand up. The raised frill makes the lizard's head look large and ferocious. It uses the same technique when fighting male rivals.

The lizard's unusual coloring acts as desert camouflage.

THORNY DEVIL

The slow-moving thorny devil, a lizard from the deserts of Australia, feeds entirely on ants. It is covered with a mass of sharp spines, making a prickly mouthful that is enough to deter most predators.

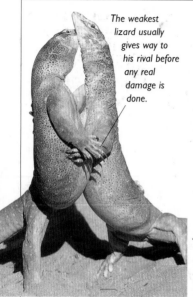

The weakest lizard usually gives way to his rival before any real damage is done.

GETTING TOGETHER

In order to mate and reproduce, reptiles need to pair up with a member of the opposite sex. Attracting a mate is the first step in reproduction. The males of some reptile species give colorful courtship displays to attract a female mate. In other species, the males fight one another for the right to mate with a female. Male reptiles also fight fiercely to defend their hunting territories. Teeth, claws, strength, and display are the weapons used in these battles between rivals.

DIRTY DANCING
These monitor lizards are called goannas in Australia. Male Gould goannas wrestle over females in the breeding season. They use their tails to balance themselves during these battles. Weight and strength bring victory.

SLOW DOWN
A male European pond tortoise scrambles onto a female's back to mate. The males have slightly concave lower shells to prevent them from slipping off.

Many tortoises mate in water.

ALL PUFFED UP

The male annole lizard displays its brightly colored throat flap to attract females. It also inflates its throat to warn other males to keep out of his territory. The largest lizard usually has the winning display.

LINKED UP

These venomous taipan snakes entwine their bodies as they mate. The male constantly flickers his tongue over the female's body.

ODD COUPLES

Male chameleons attract female mates by making jerking movements with their heads. Scientists think that some chameleon species may be all-female, and thus able to reproduce without mating with males.

The male chameleon grasps the female tightly with all four legs during mating. It uses its tail to hold on to a stem.

BREAKING OUT

TURTLE HOLES
Marine turtles bury their eggs on sandy beaches at night. The eggs are dug up by all sorts of predators, but new hatchlings are also vulnerable.

Most reptiles lay eggs. A few retain the eggs inside their bodies and give birth to fully developed, live young. Reptile eggs are white - or cream-colored. Some have a hard shell, like a bird's egg, but many have a soft shell of tough, leathery skin. Most hatchling reptiles have a sharp projection called an egg tooth which they use when breaking out of their shell.

The tortoise emerges slowly through the hole it has made.

SHELLING OUT
Tortoise eggs are laid in shallow holes dug by the female. The European tortoise lays eggs that hatch after three or four months.

It may take a long time for the tortoise to struggle out of its shell.

Egg tooth

EGG SPACE
The common iguana emerging from the shell appears too large to have fitted inside its soft-shelled egg.

While they incubate, the eggs are kept warm by the sun, or by a covering of rotting vegetation. Higher incubation temperatures tend to produce more females.

BREAKING OUT
This African spurred tortoise has split open its eggshell using the egg tooth at the end of its beak. It lies resting, eyes closed after this first effort. Its own shell and claws will harden after it has fully emerged.

The egg tooth will drop off soon after hatching.

Young tortoises have to fend for themselves and find their own food once they have hatched.

HATCHING TORTOISE
Tortoises are fully formed and independent at birth, but they are vulnerable to attack and many do not survive their first few days in the world.

Remains of the yolk sac

49

The remains of the yolk sac are attached to the tortoise's lower shell.

EARLY DAYS

Reptiles lay their eggs and leave them to hatch out on their own. King cobras are unique: they guard their eggs until they begin to hatch. Most reptiles do not need to be devoted parents because their newborn young are born mobile and able to fend for themselves. Crocodilians are the only reptiles that look after their hatchlings.

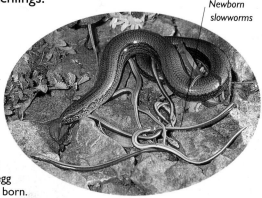

Newborn slowworms

TORTOISE FOOD

While a tortoise develops inside its egg, it is nourished by the yolk sac. When it hatches, some of the yolk sac remains attached to it for several days to provide it with a built-in food supply for one.

SLOW BABIES

Slowworms are legless lizards. The female slowworm gives birth to living young. Sometimes the babies are still encased in a soft egg sac when they are born.

BABY DRAGONS

Young bearded dragons emerge from their eggs with identical markings in a variety of different tones of color. They will rapidly disperse in all directions.

EGG THIEVES

Some snakes eat eggs. They also eat the eggs of other snakes, especially soft-shelled eggs which are easy to slit open with their sharp teeth.

A darker-colored bearded dragon

Nile crocodiles carry their young to a safe pool

CAREFUL MOTHER

A female crocodile lays her eggs in a nest, which she covers with soil and vegetation. She guards the incubating eggs and uncovers them when they start to hatch. She carries the newborn babies in her mouth to a safe pool, where she cares for them until they are independent.

FRESHEN UP

Reptile skin may wear out, or become too small for the body of a growing youngster. Many reptiles shed the outer layer of skin frequently, revealing a fresh new layer of skin beneath. Some reptile's skin slips off in one piece. Other shed their skin in flakes. Reptiles with thick scaly skin and particularly those with shells often carry a record of their periods of active feeding and growth in ridges on their shells.

CAST OFF
The common tiger snake uses rough bark to grip its old skin so that it can wriggle free. The snake emerges with a new, brighter skin color.

Just before it sheds its skin, the scales covering this snake's eyes become milky and its skin appears duller.

SKIN GLOVE
This rat snake is ready to molt. Starting at the head, the snake slowly works its way out of the old skin and leaves it behind. Because the snake has no limbs, the old skin comes off in one piece, like a glove.

TORTOISE SCALE
The ridges on a tortoise's scale or scute are created at times of rapid growth.

A NEW LOOK
The skin flakes off this lizard in large pieces. The skin covering the lizard's eyes is also renewed. The new skin is usually a little larger each time.

The molted upper skin shows the detailed pattern of scales it covered.

The young gecko has a striking yellow-and-black pattern.

NEW LOOK
The leopard gecko has bright, banded markings when it is young. As it grows to an adult, these change to a mottled brown pattern. Adult geckos shed their skin about 12 times each year.

This gecko's tail is used to store fat.

INDEX

Bobtailed Skink

Brazilian rainbow boa

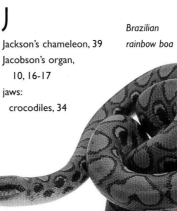

Pit viper

Tortoise